THE 12 MOST INFLUENTIAL
SPEECHES OF ALL TIME

by Marne Ventura

12 STORY
LIBRARY

Photographs ©: Mary Altaffer/AP Images, cover, 1, 27; Hulton Archive/Hulton Royals Collection/Getty Images, 5; North Wind Picture Archives, 6, 13; Currier & Ives/Library of Congress, 7, 28; Library of Congress, 8; Manuel Balce Ceneta/AP Images, 9; George Francis Schreiber/Library of Congress, 10; Carol M. Highsmith/George F. Landegger Collection of District of Columbia Photographs in Carol M. Highsmith's America Project/Carol M. Highsmith Archive/Library of Congress, 11; Frances Benjamin Johnston/Frances Benjamin Johnston Collection/Library of Congress, 14; George Grantham Bain Collection/Library of Congress, 15; National Photo Company Collection/Library of Congress, 16, 29; Dinodia Photos/Hulton Archive/Getty Images, 18; AP Images, 19, 21, 23; Cecil Stought/White House, 20; Yoichi Okamoto/White House Photo Office/LBJ Presidential Library, 22; Jack Arent/Palo Alto Daily News/AP Images, 24; KRT/Newscom, 25; Matt Dunham/AP Images, 26

Library of Congress Cataloging-in-Publication Data
A catalog record for this book is available from the Library of Congress
978-1-63235-414-3 (hardcover)   *10-5-18*
978-1-63235-485-3 (paperback)
978-1-62143-537-2 (ebook)

Printed in the United States of America
022017

Access free, up-to-date content on this topic plus a full digital version of this book. Scan the QR code on page 31 or use your school's login at 12StoryLibrary.com.

Table of Contents

Queen Elizabeth I Rallies Her Troops

In the 1580s, Spain was the world's most powerful country. Its king, Philip II, wanted to control England. England's Queen Elizabeth I did not want this to happen. This left the two countries on the brink of war.

At this time, many people felt that only men could lead a nation effectively. Elizabeth needed to convince her people and troops that she was a strong, wise leader.

THINK ABOUT IT

Does it matter if a nation's leader is a woman or a man? Has this idea changed in the years since Elizabeth was queen?

44
Number of years Queen Elizabeth I ruled England.

- King Philip II of Spain wanted to conquer England.
- Elizabeth needed to convince her army to fight for her.
- Under Elizabeth's rule, England became the world's most powerful country.

Without their support, the queen had little chance against Philip's troops. In the summer of 1588, Elizabeth expected an attack to come any day.

She spoke to her troops camped in the city of Tilbury. She told her soldiers she trusted them. She said she was willing to fight and die along with them. She said, "I know I have the body but of a weak and feeble woman; but I have the heart and stomach of a king, and of a king of England too."

Elizabeth's speech was a success. Her words convinced the soldiers

Queen Elizabeth I wanted to be on the battlefield in Tilbury, inspiring her troops to victory.

and the people of England to trust her as their leader. Spanish ships were defeated on the seas, before they reached English soil. In the years that followed, England became the world's most powerful country.

THE POWER OF SPEECH

When Elizabeth was young, she learned the art of public speaking. It added to Elizabeth's power as queen. With her speeches, Elizabeth could convince lawmakers and troops to do as she asked. She could also change public opinion in her favor. Public speaking became one of Elizabeth's most important tools as queen.

Patrick Henry Inspires a Revolution

Patrick Henry was a lawyer in the Virginia colony. Henry and other colonists had been living under England's control. In 1760, George III became king of England. He governed the colonies strictly and taxed them heavily.

King George's actions angered colonists. They felt that the high taxes were unfair. They also wanted their own government. Henry and other colonists spoke out against the king. Henry gave his most notable speech at the second Virginia Convention on March 20, 1775.

Henry hoped his speech would convince the colonists to fight King George. He said he knew the colonists were afraid of being charged with treason.

Henry also recognized that the colonists may not be able to win. But he urged them to fight. He argued that peace was not worth much without freedom. He ended with the famous phrase, "Give me liberty or give me death!"

Henry's speech motivated colonists to stand up to the British, no

Patrick Henry was a leader of the American Revolution.

matter the cost. On July 4, 1776, colonists issued the Declaration of Independence. The colonists and the British fought until 1783. That year, King George recognized the United States as an independent country. Henry's inspiring speech helped make this possible.

Patrick Henry gave his famous speech at St. John's Church in Richmond, Virginia.

29

Number of days after Patrick Henry's speech that the first shots of the American Revolution were fired.

- Patrick Henry was a lawyer and member of the second Virginia Convention.
- Colonists were unhappy with the way England's King George ruled them.
- Patrick Henry's speech convinced the colonists to begin the American Revolution.

3

Sojourner Truth Fights for Women's Rights

Sojourner Truth was born into slavery in 1797. She was freed as an adult and became a traveling preacher. Truth also wanted to end slavery and improve women's rights. At the time, women were not allowed to vote. A married woman's children and property belonged to her husband. She could not enroll in a college or university.

Truth attended the Women's Rights Convention in Akron, Ohio, in 1851. While there, she heard men speak out against women's rights. They believed women were weaker and less intelligent than men.

Other men argued that the Bible proved men were superior to women.

When she heard this, Truth wanted to respond. She had not prepared a speech, but she knew what she wanted to say. She said she was not weak. She had worked as hard as

Sojourner Truth helped former slaves go to school and find jobs.

52

Age of Isabella Baumfree when she changed her name to Sojourner Truth.

- Truth grew up in slavery.
- After becoming free, she traveled and spoke at meetings.
- She fought for women's rights and racial equality.

VERSIONS OF THE SPEECH

Sojourner Truth could not read or write. So other people recorded her speech. Several versions of the speech exist. In 1863, Frances Gage printed her version of Truth's speech. Gage gave Truth a southern accent and added the phrase "Ain't I a woman?"

any man when she was enslaved. Truth believed all people should have equal rights no matter their intelligence, skin color, or gender.

Truth's speech was short, but it had a powerful message. It raised awareness about the need for women's rights, as well as the need for an end to slavery. It also tied the need for racial equality to the women's rights movement.

First Lady Michelle Obama applauds at the unveiling of a Sojourner Truth bust at the US Capitol in 2009.

4

Frederick Douglass Champions Civil Rights

Frederick Douglass was born into slavery around 1818 in Maryland. At age 20, Douglass escaped to the North and lived as a free man. He spoke at an antislavery meeting in 1841. The speech impressed the crowd. He was soon a popular speaker at other antislavery gatherings.

In 1852, Douglass spoke to the Ladies' Anti-Slavery Society in Rochester, New York. The meeting was supposed to celebrate the Fourth of July and America's independence. But Douglass pointed out that enslaved people had not won the same independence as white people had. He told the white people in the audience, "This Fourth [of] July is yours, not mine."

Douglass went on to compare abolition to the American Revolution. He said that it seemed dangerous to change society but that it was the right thing to do. He urged his listeners to fight for racial equality. His inspiring

Frederick Douglass is often called the "Father of the Civil Rights Movement."

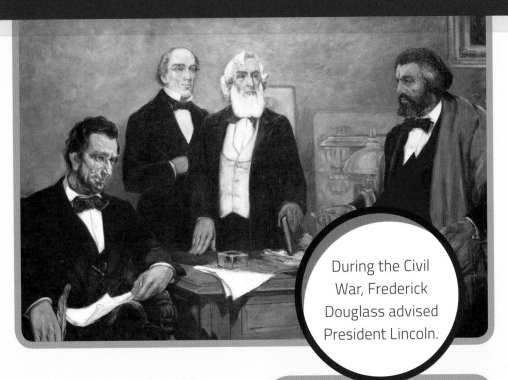

During the Civil War, Frederick Douglass advised President Lincoln.

speech became known as "What to the Slave Is the Fourth of July?"

When the Civil War began in 1861, Douglass continued to fight against slavery. His speeches and writings inspired others to join the cause. The work of Douglass and many others led to the end of slavery.

THINK ABOUT IT

What are some possible reasons Douglass spoke to an antislavery society that was composed of women? What did the women's rights movement have in common with abolition?

3.9 million
Number of enslaved people in the United States in 1860.

- Frederick Douglass grew up in slavery and became free at age 20.
- Douglass learned to read as a child even though it was illegal to teach enslaved people how to read.
- He was a civil rights speaker and was later known as the "Father of the Civil Rights Movement."

11

5

Abraham Lincoln Inspires a Nation

Abraham Lincoln became the 16th US president in 1861. He led a deeply divided nation. States in the North wanted to end slavery throughout the nation. In the South, people disagreed with this idea. They believed each state should be allowed to decide if it wanted to allow slavery or not.

A month after Lincoln took office, these disagreements led to the US Civil War. Month after month, the battles continued. Tens of thousands of soldiers died. Americans grew tired of war. Lincoln wanted to encourage people to continue fighting to end slavery. He saw an opportunity to do so after one of the war's bloodiest battles at Gettysburg, Pennsylvania.

On November 19, 1863, people gathered at Gettysburg to dedicate a cemetery for fallen soldiers. Lincoln's speech at this event became known as the "Gettysburg Address." Lincoln paid respects to the Founding Fathers and their ideals. He said the Civil War was a test to see if a nation founded on those goals could survive. He praised the fallen soldiers.

272
Number of words in the "Gettysburg Address."

- The speech paid respects to the fallen soldiers.
- It reminded Americans of the values of freedom and equality upon which the nation was founded.
- Lincoln's speech urged Americans to keep fighting for a united country.

Then Lincoln asked everyone to keep fighting for a government "of the people, by the people, and for the people."

Lincoln's speech renewed people's decreasing support for the Civil War. His words linked the Civil War to the American Revolution in its fight for freedom and equality. Today, Lincoln's speech still inspires the nation. It is one of the most quoted and memorized speeches in American history.

The "Gettysburg Address" lasted only two minutes, but it had a big impact.

Susan B. Anthony Demands Votes for Women

Susan B. Anthony was a well-educated woman from a family of political activists. She joined the women's rights movement in 1852. Anthony traveled across the country, giving speeches about women's rights. She also fought to abolish slavery.

In 1868, the US government passed the 14th Amendment. It promised equal rights to all citizens. But women were still not allowed to vote. To protest, Anthony voted in the presidential election in 1872. Two weeks later, she was arrested for voting illegally. Anthony faced a federal trial for this act.

Anthony knew her trial would have jurors who came from Monroe County, New York. She wanted to share her side of the story with potential jurors before the trial. She gave a speech called "Is It a Crime for a US Citizen to Vote?" To reach as many people as possible, she gave the speech 29 times in Monroe County. When the trial

Susan B. Anthony was a tireless voice for women's rights.

Help us to win the vote

was moved to Ontario County, she gave the speech 21 times there.

In the speech, Anthony said she did not break any law when she voted. She quoted the preamble to the Constitution, which gives liberty to the people of the United States. She argued that women are people and citizens of the United States. Therefore, she stated, women have all the same rights that men do.

Women who fought for the right to vote were known as suffragettes.

41
Number of years it took for the 19th Amendment to pass after it was proposed.

- Susan B. Anthony was an abolitionist and women's rights activist.
- She defied authorities by voting in the 1872 presidential election.
- Her speech raised awareness for the need to give women the right to vote.

And she added that the same is true for black citizens.

Despite her efforts, Anthony was found guilty at the trial. She was fined $100. That did not take away from Anthony's work. Her courage to protest the way women were treated inspired other women to stand up for their rights. In 1920, women received the right to vote when the 19th Amendment became part of the US Constitution.

Chief Joseph Addresses His People

Chief Joseph was the leader of the Nez Percé tribe in Northwest Oregon. He was known for being a peaceful leader. His people had lived in Oregon for many years. The US government ordered them to

In the Nez Percé language, Chief Joseph's name was Hin-mut-too-uah-lat-kekht, which means "Thunder Rolling in the Mountains."

move off their land to a reservation in Idaho.

Rather than fight, Chief Joseph began to move the Nez Percé. Out of anger at being forced off their land, three Nez Percé men raided a white settlement and killed several people. Chief Joseph feared the US government's reaction to the attack. So he led 800 Nez Percé to Canada to escape capture and punishment.

In June 1877, the group began traveling north. US soldiers chased and fought them across Idaho and into Montana. By the time they were nearly to Canada, almost half of the Nez Percé had been killed. The rest were hungry, cold, and tired. On October 5, 1877, US soldiers surrounded the Nez Percé in Montana's Bear Paw Mountains.

That day, Chief Joseph spoke to his people. Chief Joseph spoke in his own language. He said he was tired of fighting. He said his heart was sick and sad. He surrendered

1,170
Approximate distance, in miles (1,900 km), Chief Joseph led his people before surrendering.

- Chief Joseph was leader of the Nez Percé in northwest Oregon.
- He was leading his tribe to Canada to escape US soldiers.
- His speech ended years of war between the American Indians and white settlers.
- The US government then forced Chief Joseph's people onto a reservation.

and said, "From where the sun now stands, I will fight no more forever."

Chief Joseph's short speech ended months of fighting between the Nez Percé Indians and the US government in the West. The government forced Chief Joseph and his people onto a reservation. But Chief Joseph continued to stand up for American Indian rights.

17

Mahatma Gandhi Pushes for Independence

Mahatma Gandhi was a political leader from India. The British had ruled India since 1858. Gandhi wanted Indians to govern themselves.

On August 8, 1942, a crowd gathered in present-day Mumbai, India. A meeting of the All-India Congress Committee was taking place. Its members would decide if India would support Britain in World War II.

Gandhi spoke to the crowd. He called for nonviolent protests. He said he did not want power for himself but for the entire population of India. He wanted the people to choose their own leader. He endorsed democracy and urged Indians not to hate the British. He told people to resist British rule, even if they had to

One of Mahatma Gandhi's goals was *swaraj*, which means "self rule."

THINK ABOUT IT

How are Patrick Henry's "Give Me Liberty or Give Me Death!" speech and Gandhi's "Do or Die" speech similar? How are they different?

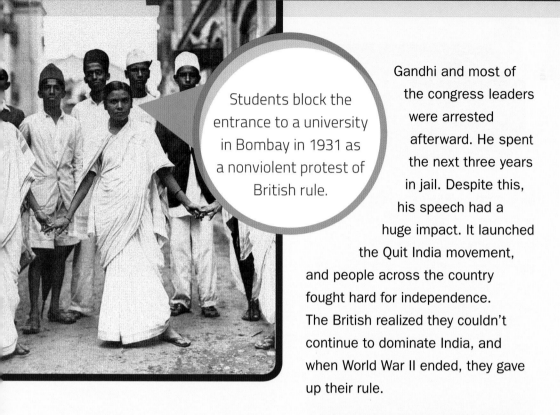

Students block the entrance to a university in Bombay in 1931 as a nonviolent protest of British rule.

Gandhi and most of the congress leaders were arrested afterward. He spent the next three years in jail. Despite this, his speech had a huge impact. It launched the Quit India movement, and people across the country fought hard for independence. The British realized they couldn't continue to dominate India, and when World War II ended, they gave up their rule.

risk their lives. Gandhi encouraged them to "do or die."

PASSIVE RESISTANCE

Gandhi's philosophy of nonviolent protest influenced other activists. Martin Luther King Jr. and other American civil rights workers used his methods to bring about change. They held peaceful sit-ins, marches, and boycotts. Malala Yousafzai also endorsed passive resistance in her call for worldwide access to education.

100,000

Approximate number of protestors released from prisons in India after it gained independence from Britain.

- Gandhi was a political leader who wanted his people to have freedom and equal rights.
- He launched the Quit India movement with his "Do or Die" speech.
- His words united the Indian people against British rule.

John F. Kennedy Challenges Americans

John F. Kennedy became the 35th US president on January 20, 1961. It was bitterly cold outside. That did not stop a large crowd from gathering at the outdoor ceremony. They wanted to watch the nation's youngest-ever president take the oath of office. After taking the oath, Kennedy gave his inaugural address. In it, he explained what he hoped to do during his term.

Kennedy had taken office during a challenging time. The United States and the Soviet Union did not get along. This period was called the Cold War. Americans feared that a possible war with the Soviet Union would

use atomic bombs. The bombs were a new form of technology. They could be launched from far away and cause mass destruction.

In his inaugural address, Kennedy spoke about this fear. He said the new technology gave the United States the power for either good or evil. His goal was to use it to show the country's strength in order to

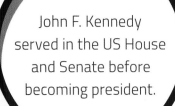

John F. Kennedy served in the US House and Senate before becoming president.

43

Kennedy's age when he became the US president.

- The Cold War was at its height when Kennedy took office.
- Kennedy wanted to use new technology for peace rather than destruction.
- He inspired many young Americans to join the Peace Corps.

avoid war. Then he asked for help from all Americans. He said, "Ask not what your country can do for you—ask what you can do for your country."

Kennedy's words changed the lives of many listeners. Thousands of young Americans joined the Peace Corps. This program's goal was to create peace and understanding among all people. The Americans who signed up agreed to live and work in other countries. They would aid the people there and make the world a better place.

Kennedy's inaugural address inspired confidence and hope in many Americans.

Lyndon B. Johnson Calls for Equal Rights

President Lyndon B. Johnson became the US president in 1963. At this time, the civil rights movement was at its height. People were actively protesting unfair treatment based on skin color.

Officials in 11 southern states were preventing black people from voting. To protest, Martin Luther King Jr. organized nonviolent marches.

On February 18, 1965, local police and Alabama state troopers shot and killed a 26-year-old protestor. King and his group marched again in Selma, Alabama, on March 7. Police and troopers brutally attacked protestors with clubs and tear gas.

In response to the attacks, Johnson spoke to Congress on March 15, 1965. He wanted Congress to pass a new law that would guarantee black people the right to vote. In his speech, he linked the marchers in Selma to the minutemen of 1775. He compared their courage to that of the soldiers who fought in World War II and the Korean War.

Lyndon B. Johnson

Lyndon B. Johnson
signs the Voting
Rights Act of 1965.

Johnson then asked Congress to pass the Voting Rights Act. It would ban officials from putting up barriers for black people when it was time to vote. When discussing this, Johnson borrowed the phrase "We shall overcome," which Martin Luther King Jr. used during his protests.

President Johnson's speech was a success. On August 6, 1965, Congress passed the Voting Rights Act. It had a deep impact on the country. More black people were registered to vote than ever before. In turn, more black officials were elected to local and national offices.

6

Percentage of black voters registered in Mississippi before in 1965.

- Black people were being denied the right to vote in 11 southern states.
- Johnson gave his speech in response to violence between protestors and police.
- President Johnson's speech helped convince Congress to pass the Voting Rights Act.

Steve Jobs Encourages Grads

Since childhood, Steve Jobs had loved electronics. He dropped out of college because he was not interested in the required courses. Instead, he wanted to follow his interest in technology. He and his friend Steve Wozniak made the first personal computer. They cofounded Apple Computer. It became one of the world's most profitable companies. Jobs and his team went on to invent the Macintosh computer, the iPod, and the iPhone.

On June 12, 2005, Jobs gave a commencement address at Stanford University in California. He gave the graduates helpful advice as they began their professional lives. Jobs said they should do what they love to do, what excites them, even if they don't know exactly where it will lead them.

In the speech, Jobs gave examples from his own life. He told them about being forced to leave Apple. At the time, it seemed terrible. But it turned out to be a good thing. He used his time away from Apple to create a new company called NeXT Inc.

As of 2016, more than 25 million people had watched Steve Jobs's commencement address at Stanford University.

1 billion

Number of iPhones sold between 2007 and 2016.

- Steve Jobs was the cofounder of Apple Computer.
- He was a college dropout who chose to follow his passion for electronics.
- His speech encouraged young people to decide their own path in life by doing what they love.

Apple later bought NeXT Inc. and rehired Jobs. The NeXT technology helped Apple create its newest products.

TOY STORY

One of Steve Jobs's projects during the years he was away from Apple was to create Pixar. Jobs bought the computer graphics division from Lucasfilm in 1986. He renamed it Pixar and began working with technology that would allow for computer-animated movies. Pixar released *Toy Story* in 1995. It was the world's first full-length movie to be animated entirely on computers.

Toy Story changed how animated movies were made.

Jobs's speech gave comfort to many of the young people starting out at an uncertain time in their lives. It gave them courage to find work they love and are good at. It encouraged them to live with uncertainty and give priority to following their interests.

Malala Yousafzai Draws Attention to Education

Malala Yousafzai was born in Pakistan in 1997. Her father ran a school there, and she was one of its students. A group called the Taliban tried to stop girls from going to school. Yousafzai began to speak against the Taliban's views about girls in school.

In 2009, Yousafzai began writing a blog for the British Broadcasting Company (BBC). In her blog entries, she worked to raise awareness of the need for education for all children. She received a Pakistan Peace Prize for her efforts in 2011.

When Yousafzai was 14, she learned the Taliban had put out a death threat for her. She was riding the bus on October 9, 2012, when a masked gunman got on board and shot Yousafzai. Yousafzai survived but was hospitalized in England until January 2013.

SCHOOL FOR GIRLS

Malala Yousafzai received the Nobel Peace Prize on December 10, 2014. She won the prize along with India's children's rights activist Kailash Satyarthi. Her prize money was more than $500,000. She donated all of it to start a secondary school for girls in Pakistan.

Malala Yousafzai is the youngest winner of the Nobel Prize for peace.

News of her attack spread around the world. More than 2 million people signed a Right to Education petition. Pakistan's assembly passed a Free and Compulsory Education Bill. When Yousafzai had recovered, she began to speak about girls' rights to education again. On July 12, 2013, she spoke at a special United Nations meeting for young people in New York.

Malala Yousafzai's first public appearance after being shot was her speech at the United Nations.

58 million

Number of children worldwide who do not have access to primary school as of 2014.

- Malala Yousafzai grew up in Pakistan, where the Taliban tried to prevent girls from going to school.
- She was shot by the Taliban for her efforts to promote education.
- Her bravery inspired others to fight for reform.

In her speech, Yousafzai called for free education for all children across the world. She said that attending school is a right all children have. Yousafzai also spoke about being shot by the Taliban. Rather than scaring her, being shot erased her fear and weakness. It made her stronger and more determined to fight.

Franklin D. Roosevelt Gives His First Inaugural Address

Roosevelt became the 32nd US president in 1933. Nearly 15 million Americans were out of work. Homeless people across the country depended on charities for food and shelter. Roosevelt's inaugural address gave people hope. He told Americans, "The only thing we have to fear is fear itself."

Ronald Reagan Demands the End of the Berlin Wall

East Germany's government built the Berlin Wall in 1961. It divided the city of Berlin. On the west side was the democratic country of West Germany. On the east side was the communist country of East Germany. President Reagan spoke in West Berlin in 1987. He challenged communist leader Mikhail Gorbachev. He said, "Mr. Gorbachev, tear down this wall!" The wall finally came down in 1989. It marked the end of the Cold War between the United States and the Soviet Union.

Michelle Obama Reminds Students to Work Hard

As First Lady of the United States, Michelle Obama was a role model for both young women and black people. In 2011, she made a speech at Oxford University. Her audience was a group of students from a girls' high school. She told them to continue their education. She talked about deciding to get her law degree at Harvard University. She told them, "I realized that if I worked hard enough I could do just as well as anyone else . . . success is not about the background you're from; it's about the confidence that you have and the effort you're willing to invest."

Glossary

abolition
The act of ending slavery.

activist
A person who takes action for political purposes.

commencement
The ceremony during which college graduates receive their degrees.

compulsory
Required by law.

endorse
To show support or approval.

juror
A person who is called upon by a court of law to decide if a person on trial is guilty or innocent.

minutemen
Citizen soldiers during the American Revolution who were ready to take part in military action at a moment's notice.

Nobel Prize
An annual award for the highest achievement in physics, chemistry, medicine, literature, peace, or economics.

reservation
An area of land reserved for use by American Indians.

treason
The crime of betraying a person's country.

For More Information

Books

Armstrong, Jennifer. *The True Story Behind Lincoln's Gettysburg Address.* New York: Aladdin, 2013.

Corey, Shana. *A Time to Act: John F. Kennedy's Big Speech.* Simon & Schuster, 2017.

Obama, Barack. *Of Thee I Sing: A Letter to My Daughters.* New York: Alfred A. Knopf, 2010.

Visit 12StoryLibrary.com

Scan the code or use your school's login at **12StoryLibrary.com** for recent updates about this topic and a full digital version of this book. Enjoy free access to:

- Digital ebook
- Breaking news updates
- Live content feeds
- Videos, interactive maps, and graphics
- Additional web resources

Note to educators: Visit 12StoryLibrary.com/register to sign up for free premium website access. Enjoy live content plus a full digital version of every 12-Story Library book you own for every student at your school.

Editor's note: The 12 topics featured in this book are selected by the author and approved by the book's editor. While not a definitive list, the selected topics are an attempt to balance the book's subject with the intended readership. To expand learning about this subject, please visit **12StoryLibrary.com** or use this book's QR code to access free additional content.

Index

About the Author

Marne Ventura is the author of 45 books for children, both nonfiction and fiction. She loves writing about history, science, technology, health, food, and arts and crafts. She and her husband live on the central coast of California.